Blast Off
to SPACE CAMP

By Lauren Weidenman

SPACE CAMP® is a registered service mark of Alabama Space Science Exhibit Commission and Alabama Space and Rocket Center. Use of this servicemark implies no sponsorship, endorsement, sale, or promotion on the part of Pearson Education, Inc.

SPACE CAMP 1-800-63 SPACE

Credits

Illustrations: 15: P.T. Pie Illustrations

Photos: All photos © Pearson Learning Group unless otherwise noted. Front cover: Richard T. Nowitz. Title page: U.S. Space Camp®. 5: NASA. 7: Bob Gathany/ U.S. Space Camp®. 8, 9: U.S. Space Camp®. 10: Robert Koropp. 11: U.S. Space Camp®. 12: Richard T. Nowitz. 13: U.S. Space Camp®. 14: NASA. 16: U.S. Space Camp®. 19: Bob Gathany/ U.S. Space Camp®. 21: Robert Koropp. 22: Richard T. Nowitz. 24: U.S. Space Camp®. 25: Robert Koropp. 27: U.S. Space Camp®. 28: Richard T. Nowitz. 29: U.S. Space Camp®. 30: Bob Gathany/ U.S. Space Camp®. 31: NASA. 33: Space Telescope Science Institute. 34: Richard T. Nowitz. 36: U.S. Space Camp®. 37: Richard T. Nowitz. 38, 39: Robert Koropp. 40: Roger Ressmeyer/Corbis. 41: Robert Koropp. 42, 44: Richard T. Nowitz. 45: D. John McCarthy/ U.S. Space Camp®. 46: Robert Koropp.

Cover and book design by Stephen Barth

ISBN 0-7652-2160-8

Printed in the United States of America

3 4 5 6 7 8 9 10   07 06 05 04 03 02

Modern Curriculum Press

Pearson Learning Group

CONTENTS

To Jim, who was interested in everything

No Ordinary Camp

Have you ever wondered what it would feel like to walk on the moon? Would you like to know what an astronaut experiences as he or she travels through space?

If so, you might be interested in visiting U.S. Space Camp®. Space Camp is no ordinary camp. It is out of this world!

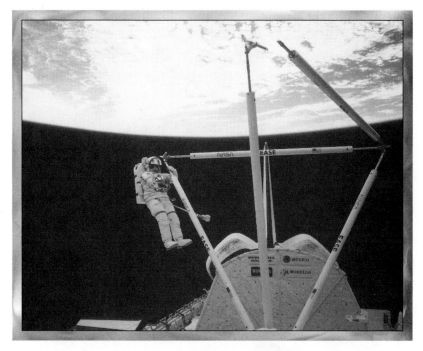

An astronaut works outside the shuttle while the spacecraft orbits Earth.

What is Space Camp?

Space Camp is a program that teaches children about space travel and exploration. It is sponsored by the U.S. Space and Rocket Center of Alabama. It is also affiliated or connected with NASA, which stands for the National Aeronautics and Space Administration. The people who work for NASA are in charge of the space shuttle and other spacecraft that travel into outer space.

The first Space Camp was started in 1982 at the U.S. Space and Rocket Center in Alabama. Now there are camps in Florida and California, and in Europe, Japan, and Canada. Each camp in the United States is located next to a major NASA center. The program is similar in all of the camps.

What happens in Space Camp?

The boys and girls who come to Space Camp are called trainees. For several action-packed days, trainees take part in many different kinds of activities. They train or practice what it is like to be an astronaut. Each trainee is treated as someone who just might have the "right stuff" to command a real NASA mission in space one day.

For a part of the week, trainees learn how it feels to be in space by using NASA training machines. For many trainees, working with these machines is just like going on rides at an amusement park. The difference is that at Space Camp the "rides" teach them something about traveling in space.

A trainee is ready to take off in the Microgravity Trainer.

Trainees learn about the history of rockets through tours of the U.S. Space and Rocket Center. They find out how space travel has changed over time.

The trainees also build their own model rockets. They work on their rockets at the beginning of camp. Then they launch the rockets on the fourth day of Space Camp.

Trainees watch special presentations, too. Some presentations take place on a special stage constructed to look like the inside of a spaceship.

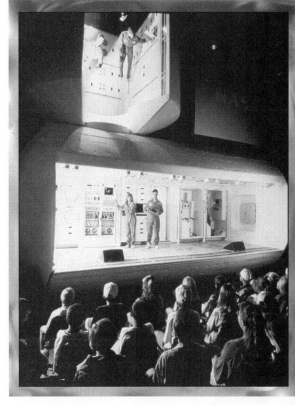

Trainees watch a performance of Outpost in Space.

A trainee works in a model of the space shuttle cockpit.

Sometimes trainees get to meet and talk with real astronauts. These men and women tell stories about training to be NASA astronauts. They talk about their experiences on space missions.

What do all these activities and training lead to?

The final project is a simulation, or a make-believe space shuttle mission. During their mission, Space Camp trainees use a special computer program to pretend that they are real members of the shuttle crew. They must work together to fly the shuttle and do the experiments and jobs that make up the mission. When their mission is completed, the trainees graduate from Space Camp on the last day.

Who can go to Space Camp?

There are no special skills needed for attending Space Camp. Anyone who is between the ages of 9 and 12 years old and in at least the fourth grade can be a Space Camp trainee. The only other "musts" are that trainees like to have fun, learn new things, and work with other kids as part of a team.

Kids arrive at Space Camp.

Space Camp Fact

More than 335,000 trainees have graduated from Space Camp in one of three places in the United States. These places are Huntsville, Alabama; Mountain View, California; and Titusville, Florida.

Life, NASA-Style

Trainees see where they will be living when they first arrive at Space Camp. The huge building is called the Space Habitat. *Habitat* means a place to live. "Wow!" is about the only thing trainees can say when they see the building. It looks like a model of a real space station.

Space Habitat

The Space Habitat is a four-story building made of huge metal tubes. The tubes are divided into sleep stations for hundreds of campers.

Life inside the habitat is a new experience for trainees. For one thing, everyday objects have different names. Water fountains are called H_2O Dispensers. The signs on the bathrooms read, "Waste Management." The sleeping areas are called bays. They are named after constellations and galaxies. Money is traded in for Space Camp money called shuttle bucks.

Space Habitat sleeping area

Trainees learn about the equipment that astronauts use.

When trainees check in, they find out which bunk they will be sleeping in and which launch team they are on. Each team has 12 members.

Trainees may choose to be fitted for a special NASA flight suit. They can wear the suit during their Space Camp Shuttle Mission at the end of the week. Other trainees may choose to wear their own clothing.

Finally, the trainees get a chance to meet their teammates and their counselors. Each team member is given a Mission Journal. In their Mission Journals they will write notes about all the new things they learn, just as astronauts do.

Now the trainees are ready to start their first activity. They are introduced to computer programs for learning about space history and technology.

The trainees learn that the space shuttle was designed to take people and equipment into outer space. The shuttle is like a complicated kind of airplane. Ordinary airplanes cannot leave the atmosphere, which is made up of the layers of air that surround Earth. The space shuttle can.

A space shuttle landing.

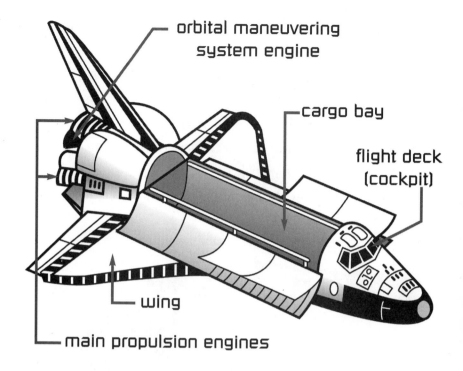

orbital maneuvering
system engine

cargo bay

flight deck
(cockpit)

wing

main propulsion engines

Orbiter

The shuttle has four main parts. These parts are the orbiter, the main engines, the solid rocket boosters, and the external tank.

The orbiter carries the crew members and their equipment. The pilot sits in the cockpit to work the controls that move the shuttle through space. The other crew members strap themselves into seats for takeoff and landing. There are also laboratory stations in the orbiter where the crew members perform experiments.

The solid rocket boosters provide the power to launch the shuttle. They push, or boost, the shuttle off the ground and away from Earth's atmosphere.

External is another word for outside. The external tank is attached to the outside of the orbiter. It's like a gas tank on a car. The external tank holds the fuel that powers the main engines.

Trainees use a computer to study the external tank and the rocket boosters that carry the shuttle into outer space.

Every space shuttle trip has a special mission, or set of jobs and experiments, to do. The overall goal of each mission is to develop ways to make space travel easier for people or to improve life on Earth.

Now it's time for the trainees to talk about their own Space Camp Shuttle Mission. They will be using a script that will tell them what to do and say. Special equipment will make it seem as though they are really flying in space.

The counselors tell the trainees about the different jobs they can do on the mission. Six trainees will be on the Flight Crew. The Flight Crew includes the commander, the pilot, and four scientists. They do experiments and different jobs both inside and outside the spacecraft. Then they have to fly the orbiter home safely.

The other six team members will make up Mission Control, or the Ground Crew. The Ground Crew communicates with the Flight Crew by computer. The flight director leads the Ground Crew. The tracking officer follows where the orbiter is in space. The orbiter systems director makes sure that all the systems on the orbiter are working. Two Ground Crew members work with scientists on the orbiter.

The campers write down three choices for the job they would like to do. Then the counselors assign jobs. The assignments are based on each trainee's interests and preferences.

Trainees are then given scripts to follow during their mission. They have to study the script carefully so that they'll know exactly what to do. During the week, they will have time to practice together before Mission Day.

Space Camp Fact

Although trainees follow a script during their mission, they may have to deal with surprise emergencies during the flight. The emergencies test how well the trainees can solve problems.

CHAPTER

3

Rockets Then and Now

Before the first day of Space Camp is over, the trainees take a tour of the Rocket Park. The first thing they see is a nearly full-size model of a space shuttle called Pathfinder. This model is about as big as a ten-story building. Seeing the shuttle firsthand makes it easier for the trainees to understand how the different parts of the shuttle work together.

Model of the space shuttle Pathfinder

In the Rocket Park, trainees also see real rockets from the United States and other countries. They learn about the ways in which rockets have changed, from the earliest models to today's more modern missiles.

The trainees also find out that there are two kinds of rocket engines. The space shuttle uses both. One kind of engine burns solid fuel. The two rocket boosters that lift the space shuttle off the ground are solid-fuel rocket engines. When their fuel is gone, they separate from the shuttle. Then they float down to the ocean on parachutes.

The other kind of rocket engine burns liquid fuel. The speed at which these engines use up their fuel can be controlled. It's just like pushing the gas pedal on a car. They are used as main engines instead of boosters. The three main engines that power the space shuttle's flight are liquid-fuel rocket engines.

The trainees also get a look at the Saturn V. This is the largest rocket in the world. Saturn V is one of the original rockets that provided the power to send astronauts Neil Armstrong and Buzz Aldrin to the moon in 1969.

A trainee is standing in one of the
Saturn V's five engines.

Saturn V is about 36 stories tall when standing upright. The original Saturn V now lies on the ground. Looking at the bottom end of the rocket, trainees can see the ends of its five huge booster engines. The engines are so large that a trainee can stand inside one of them. Each engine used up 5,000 gallons of fuel per second to send the Apollo module to the moon.

There is also a full-size model of the Saturn V that stands upright. Trainees can examine all parts of the original rocket as it lies on its side. They can also see how enormous the model looks as it stands up.

After the tour the trainees return to Habitat. There they get the kits they will use to build their own model rockets. The trainees have to begin working on the rockets right away. They need to have them ready for the launch on Day Four.

Space Camp trainees work on their model rockets.

In their role as engineers, Space Camp trainees have to look at every little detail when they build their rockets. They need to follow the directions very carefully.

The rockets that the trainees build are powered by one solid-fuel rocket engine. This engine lifts the rocket off the ground and up into the air.

As the rocket soars into the air, exhaust gases from the single engine are building up inside the rocket. When the gases have built up enough pressure, they pop out a plug in the rocket. This plug holds a small parachute inside the rocket. When the plug pops out, the parachute is pushed out of the rocket. The parachute fills with air and the rocket floats down onto the grass.

Space Camp Fact

Space Camp trainees are rated in all of the activities. They are rated on how well they follow directions and on how well they work with others as a team.

Fasten Your Seat Belts

On Day Two trainees get a chance to work with some of the NASA training equipment. Part of the equipment is a model of the Apollo Command Module Mission Simulator. The Apollo missions carried astronauts to the moon from 1969 to 1972. The Command Module of the Apollo spacecraft was where the crew lived and did most of the work while in space.

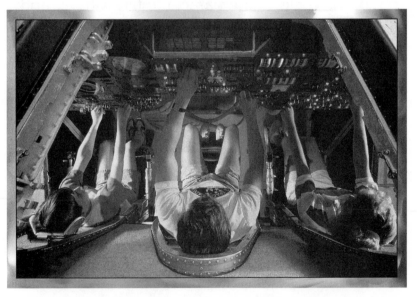

Apollo Command Module Mission Simulator

A trainee tries out the Microgravity Trainer.

Though the module was small, three astronauts spent up to 12 days inside it. Most of the time they were sitting or lying on narrow couches. The space shuttle orbiter has much more room for astronauts to move around.

Trainees get a chance to feel what it's like to walk on the moon with a simulator called the 1/6th Gravity Chair or Microgravity Trainer. Bouncing in the chair, a trainee feels nearly weightless!

Gravity is the force that holds things down on Earth's surface. It gives things weight. The gravity on the moon is one sixth that of Earth. So a person who weighed 96 pounds on Earth would weigh only 16 pounds on the moon!

It is important for astronauts to know what it feels like to weigh so little. The main difference is that it takes very little effort to move. The energy normally used to take a step on Earth could send a person bouncing out of control on the moon.

In the 1/6th Gravity Chair, astronauts can practice moving. The chair hangs from the ceiling by a special spring that helps a person feel the level of gravity on the moon. A person sitting in the chair can bounce really high or move forward just by gently pushing off the floor.

On the moon there is a little gravity, but in space there is almost none at all. The Five Degrees of Freedom Chair is used to teach astronauts how to move around in the weightlessness of space. This machine is especially useful for training the Mission Specialists who will work outside the spacecraft.

The chair glides on air. Trainees sitting in the chair are pitched and tossed. They feel as though they are tumbling through space with nothing to grab onto. Using this chair helps trainees understand how important it is for astronauts to properly attach themselves to the spacecraft while they are working outside.

Another simulator that helps train Mission Specialists for their work outside the spacecraft is the Manned Maneuvering Unit, or the MMU. This machine is attached like a backpack. It allows an astronaut to fly freely in space without any connection to the spacecraft at all.

Five Degrees of Freedom Chair

Manned
Maneuvering
Unit
simulator

To control the MMU, the trainee learns how to use the switches in the arms of the unit. These will move the unit in any direction.

Space Camp trainees use the MMU simulator even though MMUs have not been used in real space missions since 1994. No one was ever hurt using an MMU. NASA decided that a space walk with no connection to the shuttle was just too dangerous.

Training underwater in a large pool also helps trainees learn about weightlessness in space. The water supports some of the trainees' weight. As a result, they can move more freely, as though the force of gravity were not as strong.

In the water, trainees also practice how to get out of the spacecraft when there is an emergency. They pretend to enter the orbiter by swimming through hoops.

A spin on the Multi-Axis Trainer sends trainees tumbling in all directions at top speed. In this machine, trainees feel what it would be like to tumble head-over-heels inside a spacecraft that is spinning out of control.

Multi-Axis Trainer

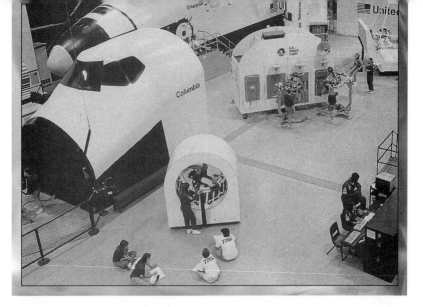

Space Camp Training Center

Even though the NASA training machines are fun to use, they teach important lessons. With these machines, trainees can learn from their experiences "in space" without ever having to leave the ground.

Space Camp Fact

Astronauts' bodies can change as a result of being in space. In less gravity there is less pressure on bodies. Some astronauts have temporarily become an inch or so taller because their spines have become longer and straighter!

Fast-Forward to the Future

On Day Three, trainees step into the future. They find out how people are planning to live in space someday. The day begins with a trip to NASA's Marshall Space Flight Center. There the trainees see a model of the International Space Station. NASA and scientists from other countries are developing the station.

An artist's drawing of the International Space Station

The International Space Station is being built in space as a place where people can live and work for several months at a time. It will have laboratories, work areas, and living areas for six to eight crew members.

The living areas are housed in a part of the space station called the Habitation Module. The module has a space for each crew member to sleep. Inside each space is a sleeping bag attached to the wall. It doesn't matter where the sleeping bag is because there is almost no gravity in space. This means there is no sense of up or down. So sleeping against a wall feels exactly the same as sleeping on the floor or on the ceiling.

On the wall near the sleeping bag is a built-in stereo headset. Some areas may even have laptop computers to receive and send e-mail. Each space is small, so the astronauts do not have much room to move around.

Crew members on the space station will use exercise machines to help their muscles and bones stay strong. There are also kitchen areas where the astronauts can prepare food. Meals are in special packages that can be heated in a microwave oven. Without the special packages, weightless globs of food and liquids might get loose and drift around the cabin.

Scientists started building the International Space Station in 1998. They are using the space shuttle to transport the station into space, one piece at a time. Parts have already been put together by scientists with the help of robots.

An astronaut working in outer space

Forty-four separate space shuttle launches will be needed to complete the space station by 2004. At that point the space station could be used as a base for building other space stations that will be located farther out in space. It could also be used as a refueling stop for future space missions.

The trainees return to Space Camp after the visit to the Space Flight Center. They are ready for their next adventure. The setting will be Space Camp's own Mars base in the Rocket Park. The trainees will pretend to be astronauts exploring Mars.

A trainee wears a spacesuit while working on a project.

Trainees work together to set up a model of a space base and shelter. They inspect a model of the Space Camp Surveyor, a machine designed to map the surface of planets. They also collect soil samples and rocks. The trainees write a description of each sample and seal it in a plastic bag to send back to Earth.

 **Space Camp Fact**

The spacecraft Lunar Prospector may have detected ice on the moon. Ice is water in its solid form. If there is ice on the moon, the ice could someday provide the water and oxygen needed for a human colony.

The Rocket Launch

On July 20, 1969, NASA astronaut Neil Armstrong became the first person to step on the moon. He said, "That's one small step for man, one giant leap for mankind." Then he showed the people watching television back on Earth what it was like to walk and hop on the moon. It was an exciting day for all people.

A counselor helps trainees prepare their rockets for launch.

Model rockets lifting off

Day Four of Space Camp is just as exciting for the trainees. It's Rocket Launch Day. The trainees gather with their teammates at the launch site to watch their rockets blast off. They have done their best during the week to build the rockets well. Now they will see whether their rockets will fly.

For safety reasons, a counselor loads each rocket with its rocket engine. The engine contains solid fuel that burns easily. It could cause a fire if not handled in the right way.

Finally it is time for the rockets to be launched. The trainees go behind a protective barrier to stay away from flying sparks. They hope their rockets will soar, then float down and land gently.

The rockets are launched one at a time. First comes the countdown. Then someone yells "Fire!" The booster engines are lit, and the rocket shoots up into the air, trailing a cloud of smoke.

No sooner is each rocket in the air when out bursts the parachute. It fills with air. The trainees are happy to see the parachute pop open. That means the rockets work correctly.

Trainees run to pick up their rockets.

A model rocket floats to the ground.

The trainees charge onto the field to find their own capsules as soon as the last team member's rocket lands in the grass. They cannot wait to see how their capsule survived its journey.

During Space Camp training, the counselors tell the trainees that exploring space can be a risky adventure. The trainees have to be ready for any outcome, good or bad. This attitude helps to prepare them for possible disappointments. Some rockets misfire. Usually, the rockets fly well, and the trainees feel great about the fine job they've done.

That evening the trainees watch the film *Hail Columbia!* The star of the movie is one of America's first space shuttles, the Columbia. The trainees watch carefully. They don't forget for a second that their own space shuttle mission is scheduled for the next day. The name of their Space Camp space shuttle is also Columbia!

Space shuttle Columbia on the launching pad

 Space Camp Fact

The Columbia space shuttle was named after the first U.S. Navy ship to circle the globe. Columbia was also the name of the command module for *Apollo 11*, the first mission to land on the moon.

Mission Day

On the morning of Day Five, trainees are ready to begin their mission. They have rehearsed their parts for Mission Day, and they know what to do. The only thing they don't know is what in-flight emergencies they may experience.

The trainees on the Mission Control team take their seats and put on their headphones. The Flight Crew team members board the Columbia and fasten their seat belts. With earphones on, they check their monitors. They are ready.

Flight Crew team members

The Space Camp mission program is loaded into the computer. The computer screens show the space shuttle ready and waiting on the launch pad. Now it is up to the trainees to make something happen.

Flying a space shuttle takes concentration.

The first line is spoken by the flight director in Mission Control. He or she tells the Flight Crew that final preflight checks have been completed. The pilot replies that all systems are ready. Then the countdown begins: "T-minus 10 seconds...8, 7. Main engine start. 3, 2, 1, booster ignition."

Blast off! With a deafening roar, Columbia's booster engines fire. The shuttle on the computer monitor bursts free of the launch pad. It soars into the sky. As the shuttle climbs upward, its solid rocket boosters separate and fall away. Then the external fuel tank does the same. Soon Columbia is in orbit, and no rockets are needed. The orbiter is bound by gravity to circle around Earth.

The trainees in the shuttle model never leave the ground. However, the computer program is so realistic that they really feel as though they are flying into space.

Once the Columbia is in orbit, the mission specialists put on their spacesuits to do their jobs outside the spacecraft. These jobs are called extravehicular activities, or EVAs. The trainees use one of the simulators they had trained on earlier in the week to do the EVAs.

Mission Control team members

One of these machines is the 5DF, the Five Degrees of Freedom chair. Attached to the spacecraft, the 5DF Chair is used for jobs outside the space shuttle Columbia. One job is refilling the shuttle's fuel tank.

The trainees know that an emergency could happen at any moment. They try to concentrate on what they are doing. They have been told how to deal with certain types of emergencies in their Space Camp training. One of these might be a computer failure or some kind of mechanical problem.

Other emergencies are new to the trainees. One example would be a fuel leak in one of the shuttle's engines. Then the commander would be offered options on the computer screen. The commander could choose to cancel experiments to save fuel. He or she might wait for a rescue shuttle. The commander could also shut down the bad engine and try to get by with the remaining fuel. The commander has to think quickly.

Space camp trainees will most likely complete their mission successfully if they know their scripts and handle any in-flight emergencies well. They know they have done it the moment the trainees hear their flight director say, "Welcome home and congratulations on a job well done." Their mission is accomplished.

When a mission is successfully completed, it's time to celebrate.

On the morning of their sixth day, the trainees graduate from Space Camp. The ceremony begins with a few words from a guest speaker. Sometimes it is a real astronaut.

The speaker tells the trainees to follow their dreams for the future. He or she advises the trainees to take math and science in school if they want to be astronauts. Trainees also find out that the science of space exploration in the future may include discoveries and inventions. There will also be jobs that no one today can even imagine.

A trainee graduates from Space Camp.

Then the trainees are called up by teams. They are given their graduation certificates. They are also given silver Space Camp pins. The pins are shaped like pairs of outstretched wings. The trainees are proud of themselves. They have done a good job. U.S. Space Camp has helped them reach out into space and into the future.

Space Camp Fact

Some people who work at NASA today attended Space Camp when they were younger. Carlos Garcia Galan went to the Space Academy, a camp for kids in high school. Afterward, he decided to make space science his career. He is now a flight controller for electrical power systems for the International Space Station. He plans to work on the Space Station itself someday.

GLOSSARY

astronaut   [AS truh naht]   a person trained to operate spacecraft and fly into outer space

cockpit   [KAHK piht]   in a large aircraft, the space where the pilot and co-pilot sit

emergencies   [ih MUR jun seez]   sudden happenings that need attention right away

experiments   [ihk SPER uh munts]   tests to find out how something works or to see if a theory is correct

laboratory   [LAB ruh tor ee]   a place where scientific work is done

misfire   [MIHS fyr]   fail to go off; fail to work right

missiles   [MIHS ulz]   objects made to be hurled or shot toward a target

mission   [MIHSH un]   a special duty that a person or group is sent to do

script   [skrihpt]   a copy of a play or program used by those who will be performing it

simulation   [sihm yoo LAY shun]   make-believe; an event that is only pretend, not real